W9-BCA-720

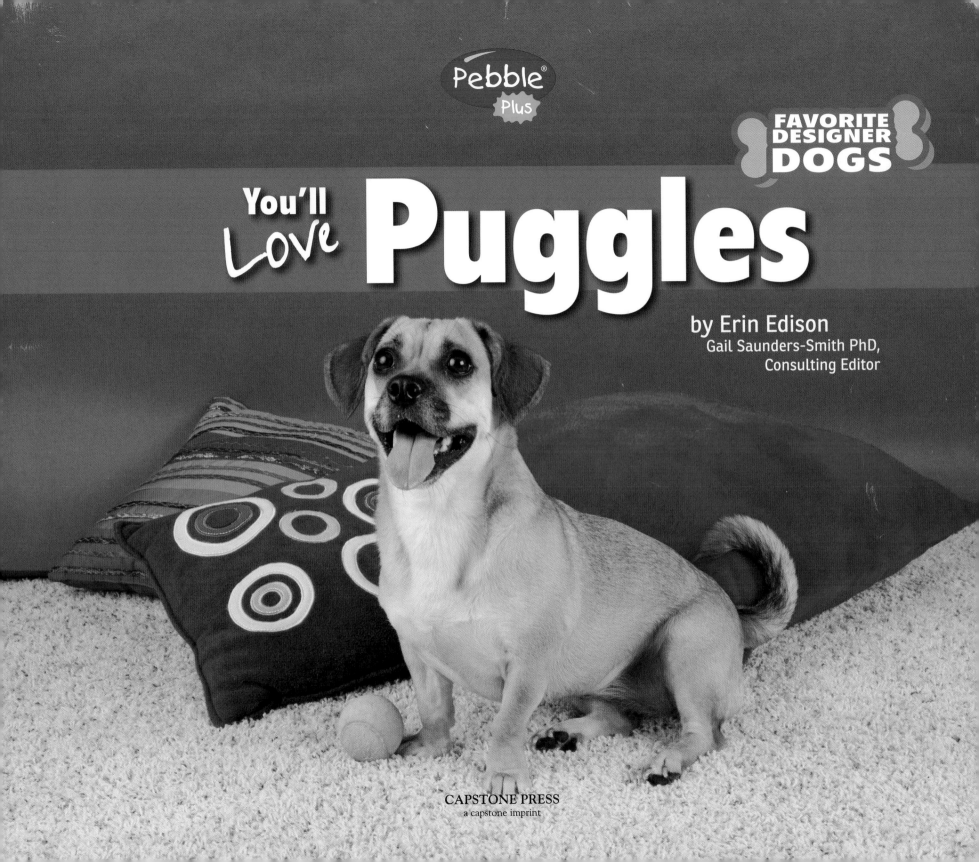

Pebble® Plus

FAVORITE DESIGNER DOGS

You'll Love **Puggles**

by Erin Edison

Gail Saunders-Smith PhD,
Consulting Editor

CAPSTONE PRESS
a capstone imprint

Pebble Plus is published by Capstone Press,
1710 Roe Crest Drive, North Mankato, Minnesota 56003
www.capstonepub.com

Copyright © 2015 by Capstone Press, a Capstone imprint. All rights reserved. No part of this publication may be reproduced in whole or in part, or stored in a retrieval system, or transmitted in any form or by any means, electronic, mechanical, photocopying, recording, or otherwise, without written permission of the publisher.

Library of Congress Cataloging-in-Publication Data
Edison, Erin, author.
  You'll love puggles / Erin Edison.
    pages cm.—(Favorite designer dogs) (Pebble plus)
  Includes bibliographical references and index.
  ISBN 978-1-4914-0572-7 (hb)—ISBN 978-1-4914-0640-3 (pb)—ISBN 978-1-4914-0606-9 (eb)
1. Puggle—Juvenile literature. 2. Toy dogs—Juvenile literature. 3. Dog breeds—Juvenile literature. I. Title. II. Title: You will love puggles.
  SF429.C49E35 2015
  636.76—dc23

  2014001835

Editorial Credits
Erika L. Shores, editor; Kyle Grenz, designer; Katy LaVigne, production specialist

Photo Credits
Capstone Studio: Karon Dubke, 1, 7, 9, 17, 19; Shutterstock: Alexia Khruscheva, 5, AnetaPics, 11, Anna Hoychuk, cover, 21, Eric Isselee, 5, Rick's Photography, 15; SuperStock: Beate Zoeller/F1 ONLINE, 13

Design Elements
Shutterstock: Julynx

Note to Parents and Teachers

The Favorite Designer Dogs series supports national science standards related to life science. This book describes and illustrates puggles, a cross between a pug and a beagle. The images support early readers in understanding the text. The repetition of words and phrases helps early readers learn new words. This book also introduces early readers to subject-specific vocabulary words, which are defined in the Glossary section. Early readers may need assistance to read some words and to use the Table of Contents, Glossary, Read More, Internet Sites, and Index sections of the book.

Printed in the United States of America in North Mankato, Minnesota.
042014   008087CGF14

Table of Contents

What Is a Puggle?

Playful puggles are designer dogs. Designer dogs are a mix of two breeds. A pug and a beagle make up a puggle.

pug

beagle

Puggles are happy and loyal. They do best in homes with owners who play with them.

The Puggle Look

Puggles are mid-sized dogs.
Adult puggles weigh 15 to
30 pounds (7 to 14 kilograms).
They stand 10 to 15 inches
(25 to 38 centimeters) tall.

Puggles have wrinkly foreheads
and curled tails like pugs.
Their long, floppy ears
come from the beagle.

Some puggles are black.

Other puggles are multi-colored.

They can have black and tan

markings. They can also have

black, tan, and white markings.

Puppy Time

Every puggle puppy is different.

Some puggles are calm

and act more like pugs.

Others are full of energy

like beagles.

15

Caring for Puggles

Puggles should be fed twice each day. Food gives them energy to play.

Take a puggle for a checkup once a year. Veterinarians look at the dog's ears, eyes, teeth, and coat. With good care, puggles live 12 to 14 years.

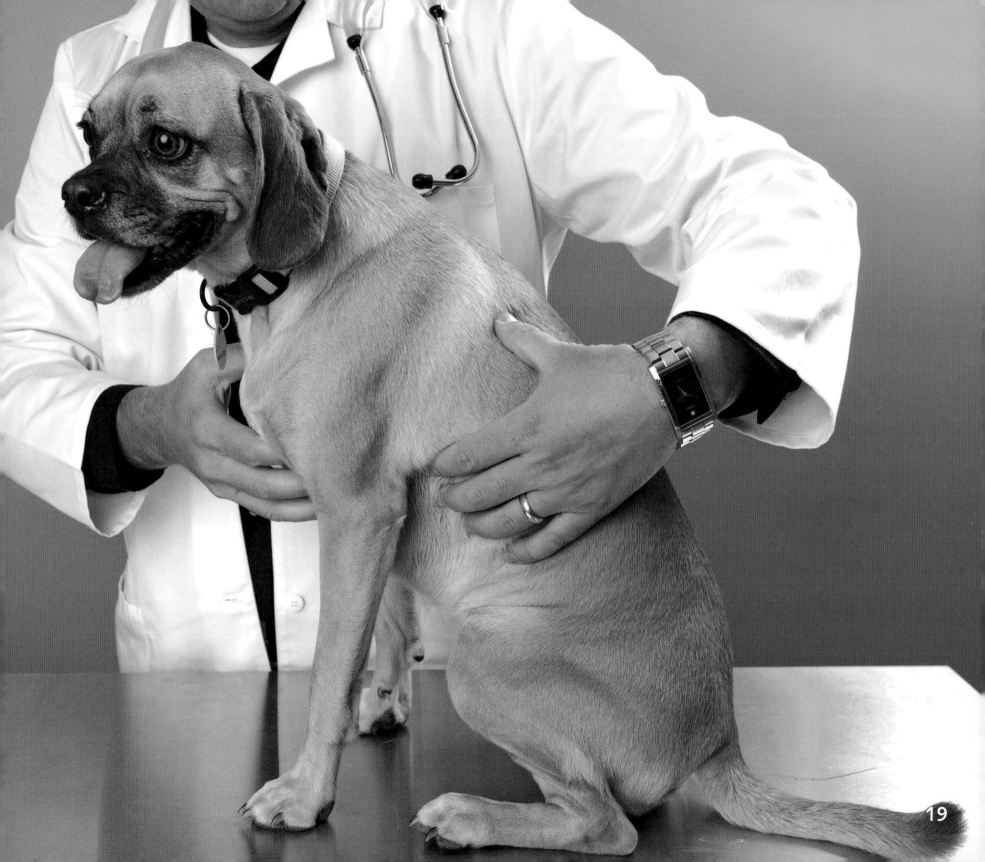

A Loving Pup

Puggles make great family pets.

They are gentle with children.

Puggles are full of love

for their owners.

Glossary

breed—a certain kind of animal within an animal group

energy—the strength to do active things without getting tired

loyal—being true to something or someone

markings—patches of color on fur

veterinarian—a doctor who treats sick or injured animals; veterinarians also help animals stay healthy

Read More

Ganeri, Anita. *Ruff's Guide to Caring for Your Dog.* Pets' Guides. Chicago: Capstone Heinemann Library, 2013.

Owen, Ruth. *Puggles.* Designer Dogs. New York: PowerKids Press, 2013.

Shores, Erika L. *All About Beagles.* Dogs, Dogs, Dogs. North Mankato, Minn.: Capstone Press, 2013.

Internet Sites

FactHound offers a safe, fun way to find Internet sites related to this book. All of the sites on FactHound have been researched by our staff.

Here's all you do:

Visit *www.facthound.com*

Type in this code: 9781491405727

Check out projects, games and lots more at
www.capstonekids.com

Index

Word Count: 185
Grade: 1

Early-Intervention Level: 15